W9-BQL-753

A TRUE BOOK™

Saturn

ELAINE LANDAU

Children's Press®
A Division of Scholastic Inc.
New York Toronto London Auckland Sydney
Mexico City New Delhi Hong Kong
Danbury, Connecticut

Content Consultant

Michelle Yehling

Astronomy Education Consultant

Aurora, Illinois

Reading Consultant

Linda Cornwell

Literacy Consultant

Carmel, Indiana

Library of Congress Cataloging-in-Publication Data

Landau, Elaine.
 Saturn / by Elaine Landau.
     p. cm.—(A true book)
 Includes bibliographical references and index.
 ISBN-13: 978-0-531-12567-0 (lib. bdg.)   978-0-531-14795-5 (pbk.)
 ISBN-10: 0-531-12567-X (lib. bdg.)   0-531-14795-9 (pbk.)
 1. Saturn (Planet)—Juvenile literature. I. Title. II. Series.
 QB671.L362 2008
 523.46—dc22   2007004181

All rights reserved. Published in 2008 by Children's Press, an imprint of Scholastic Inc.
Published simultaneously in Canada. Printed in the United States of America.
SCHOLASTIC, CHILDREN'S PRESS, A TRUE BOOK, and associated logos are trademarks and/or registered trademarks of Scholastic Inc.
1 2 3 4 5 6 7 8 9 10 R 17 16 15 14 13 12 11 10 09

Find the Truth!

Everything you are about to read is true *except* for one of the sentences on this page.

Which one is **TRUE**?

T or F   Saturn's rings are one solid piece.

T or F   If you tried to stand on Saturn, you would sink into the planet.

Find the answer in this book.

Contents

THE BIG TRUTH!

History of the Mystery

A person who weighs 100 pounds on Earth would weigh about 91 pounds on Saturn.

A space probe took this photo of the surface of Titan, Saturn's largest moon.

Saturn

Unlike stars, Saturn does not
create its own light. The light
we see is sunlight that bounces
off of the planet.

CHAPTER 1

A Trip to Saturn

You can see Saturn without a telescope.

Saturn looks like a bright star in Earth's night sky. Through a telescope, you can see its shining rings. People have admired this beautiful planet for hundreds of years. Some people call Saturn the jewel of our **solar system**.

Imagine that you could blast off in a spaceship and travel to Saturn. It would be a long trip. You would be in your spaceship for at least three years. But you would have plenty to see along the way.

You would see thousands of stars once you rose above Earth's **atmosphere**. An atmosphere is a blanket of gases that surrounds a planet or a moon. The stars would look much brighter than they do from Earth. You might also spot Mars and Jupiter as you flew through space. You would be moving away from the sun as you flew toward Saturn. So the sun would appear to get smaller.

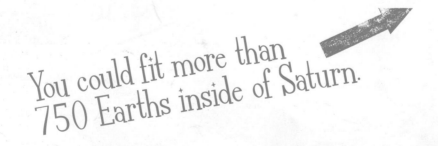

You could fit more than 750 Earths inside of Saturn.

As you flew toward Saturn
in a spaceship, Earth would
slowly seem to shrink until
it looked like a blue dot.

As you neared Saturn, you would see its frozen, yellow and white clouds. Saturn is a giant planet. But you wouldn't find a place to land your spaceship. That's because Saturn has no solid surface to land on. Below its clouds, Saturn is mostly liquid and gas. You would sink. That's just one of the problems you would find if you tried to visit the "jeweled planet."

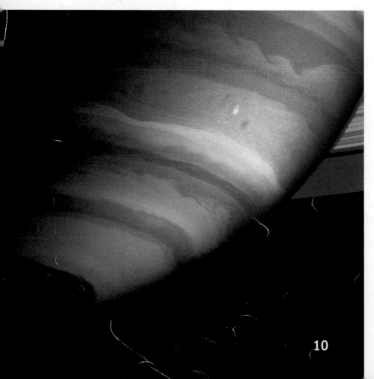

The colors in this photo were changed to show the different heights of Saturn's clouds. The highest clouds are gray. The red clouds are deep in Saturn's atmosphere.

Who Was Saturn?

The ancient Romans named the planet Saturn after their god of farming. The Romans believed that Saturn taught people how to farm. Saturn was also the Roman god of time.

Every December, ancient Romans held a festival called *Saturnalia* in Saturn's honor. For a week, people held feasts and gave gifts to one another. The day of the week we call Saturday is also named after Saturn.

Ancient Romans celebrated Saturnalia.

This drawing shows the sun
lighting up Saturn's rings. In
reality, the sun would appear
much smaller from Saturn.

CHAPTER 2

Saturn in the Solar System

The 3 planets nearest to Saturn have rings too. But Saturn's rings are the biggest and brightest.

Our solar system is like a neighborhood in space. Planets **orbit**, or travel around, the sun. Saturn's closest neighbors are Jupiter, Uranus, and Neptune. Four other planets orbit closer to the sun. Turn the page to see them all.

Saturn's Solar System

Pluto (dwarf planet)

Uranus

Mars

Mercury

Jupiter

asteroid belt

Saturn

- Sixth planet from the sun
- Second-largest planet
- Diameter: About 75,000 mi. (120,700 km)
- One day equals about 10 hours, 47 minutes on Earth
- One year equals 30 Earth years

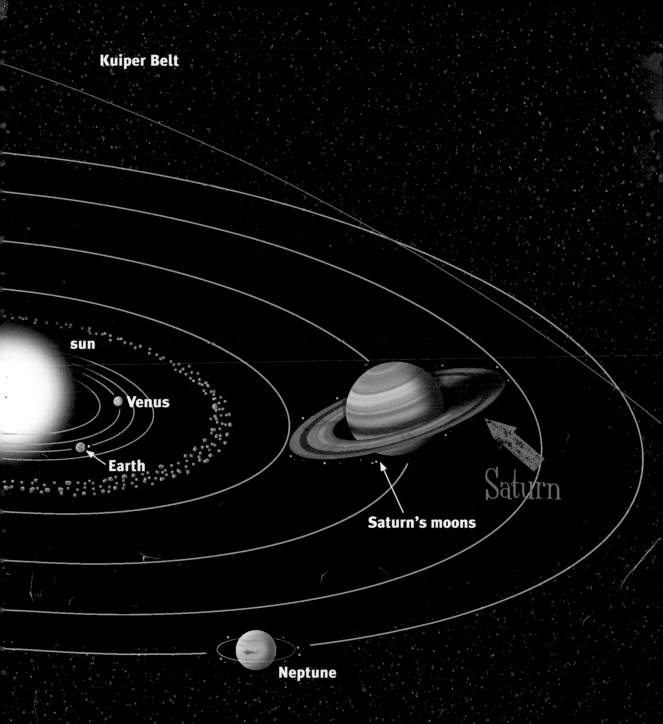

Kuiper Belt

sun

Venus

Earth

Saturn's moons

Saturn

Neptune

15

Comet Hale-Bopp ⟶

Icy comets, such as this one, orbit the sun along with the planets.

Saturn on the Move

Some planets travel farther than others to complete one orbit. Saturn is the sixth planet from the sun. Earth is the third. So Saturn has a larger orbit.

Saturn travels this large orbit at a very slow speed. The time it takes a planet to complete its orbit is called the planet's year. A year on Saturn is the same as about 30 years on Earth!

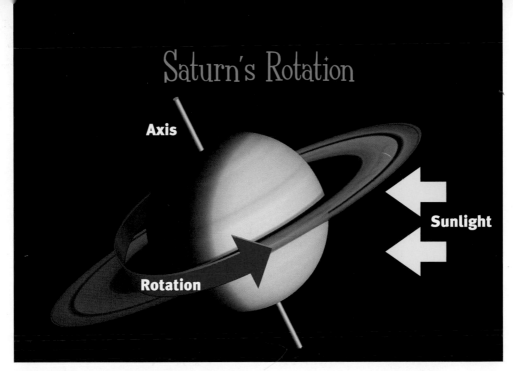

Saturn's Rotation

Axis

Sunlight

Rotation

The red arrow in this diagram shows the direction of Saturn's rotation. It is daytime on the side that faces the sun. As the planet rotates, new parts move into the sunlight.

As a planet orbits, it also spins on its **axis**. An axis is an imaginary line that runs from north to south through the center of a planet. A planet's day is equal to one full **rotation**, or spin, on its axis.

Saturn spins on its axis very quickly—much faster than Earth. So a day on Saturn is equal to about 10 hours, 47 minutes on Earth.

This image was taken by the *Cassini* spaceship. It shows the bands of clouds that blow in circles around Saturn.

CHAPTER 3

What Is Saturn Made Of?

Saturn's interior is always hidden by clouds.

Think about Earth's surface. Is it made of rock? Could you land a spaceship on it? The answer to these questions is yes. But for Saturn, the answer to these questions is no.

Glowing lights, or auroras, swirl above Saturn's north and south poles. The auroras can only be seen from space.

Scientists know that Saturn has no solid surface. They call Saturn a "gas giant." A gas giant is a big planet made mostly of gas and liquid. Jupiter, Uranus, and Neptune are gas giants, too.

Jupiter is so large that all the other planets could fit inside it.

Jupiter is the largest gas giant. People sometimes call it "the king of the planets."

What's in the Air?

Saturn has a thick, cloudy atmosphere. This atmosphere is very different from that of Earth. Earth's atmosphere contains a **chemical** called oxygen, which people need to breathe. Saturn's atmosphere has no oxygen to breathe. The atmosphere, the frozen clouds above it, and the rest of the planet are made mostly of the same chemical—hydrogen. It is difficult for **astronomers** to know where Saturn's atmosphere ends and the liquid layer begins.

If you look at Saturn's clouds, you see thick, yellow and white bands. People say that it looks like a piece of lemon meringue pie. You would not want to get close to this "pie," however. The clouds contain gases that are poisonous to people. These gases are called ammonia and methane.

An artist drew this picture of Saturn as it might look from one of its moons.

If a spaceship entered Saturn's atmosphere, the tremendous pressure would crush it like a can.

Inside Saturn

Saturn's heavy atmosphere puts pressure on the planet. You don't notice it, but the atmosphere on Earth presses down on our planet, too. Saturn's pressure is much higher than Earth's.

Saturn's atmosphere squeezes the planet itself. This pressure turns much of the hydrogen gas inside the planet into liquid. At its core, Saturn is made of solid rock.

Enormous pressure at Saturn's center causes the temperature there to be very high. Saturn's core may be hotter than the sun's surface!

How Is the Weather?

When the freezing-cold winds die down to 50 miles (80 km) per hour, that is a good-weather day on Saturn. Fast, strong winds keep Saturn's clouds swirling all the time. The winds at Saturn's **equator** can reach speeds of 1,100 miles (1,770 km) per hour.

Some of Saturn's storms are so large they can be seen from space.

The bright spot on Saturn is a huge storm.

Winds of 50 miles (80 km) per hour would be good weather on Saturn. On Earth, it would be a very windy day!

The strongest tornadoes on Earth have only reached speeds of about 300 miles (483 km) per hour. But even those winds have destroyed houses and ruined towns.

Saturn is much farther from the sun than Earth. So Saturn receives much less sunlight. The temperature of its clouds can go as low as –218 degrees Fahrenheit (–139 degrees Celsius). Cold temperatures freeze the gases in the atmosphere. The yellow and white clouds we see are frozen particles of ice.

Saturn has its own source of heat, however. Its core is superhot! That causes Saturn to give off more than twice as much heat as it receives from the sun!

1856

Scottish scientist James Clerk Maxwell suggests that the rings are made of many small pieces.

1980-81

The space probes *Voyager 1* and *Voyager 2* take photos proving that Saturn has thousands of rings made of small pieces.

2004

The *Cassini* (kah-SEE-nee) spaceship and the space probe *Huygens* (HY-guhnz) investigate Saturn and its rings (shown below). The rings are grouped into several main sections. They've been given names of letters of the alphabet, in order of their discovery.

History of the Rings

Since astronomers first saw Saturn with a telescope, they have been fascinated by the planet's rings. Follow this timeline to see how the rings were discovered.

1610

Italian astronomer Galileo uses his telescope to observe Saturn and its rings. He describes the rings as "ears" or "handles."

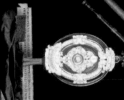

1656

Dutch astronomer Christiaan Huygens determines that the "ears" or "handles" are actually rings around Saturn.

1837

German astronomer Johann Franz Encke discovers a third ring around Saturn.

27

This illustration shows some of the rock and ice that make up Saturn's rings.

CHAPTER 4

Icy Rings

Some rocks found in Saturn's rings may be from smashed moons.

Saturn has thousands of rings. From far away, the rings look like one solid piece. If you could get close, however, you would see that they are not one piece. The rings are made of billions of pieces of ice and rock. These pieces are all different sizes. Some are as small as a grain of sand. Others are the size of a house.

Saturn is not the only planet in the solar system with rings. Jupiter, Uranus, and Neptune have them, too. No planet has as many as Saturn does, though.

While Saturn orbits the sun, Saturn's rings orbit Saturn. Every particle in every ring has its own orbit. Each ring orbits at a different speed. The rings are held in orbit by Saturn's **gravity**. Gravity is the force that pulls two objects together. The sun's gravity pulls on the planets and keeps them from shooting out into space.

Astronomers think that Saturn's ring material comes from shattered moons, **comets**, and **asteroids**. Astronomers believe that Saturn's rings are not as old as the planet. They think the rings constantly break apart and new rings form.

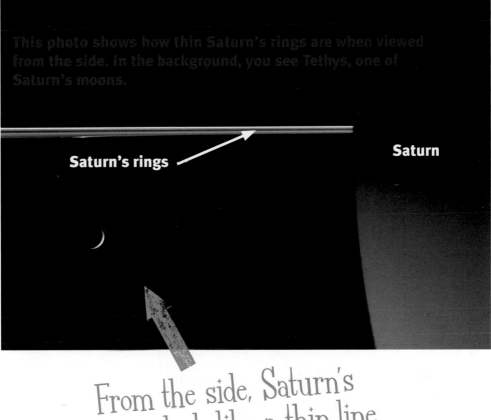

Saturn's rings

Saturn

From the side, Saturn's rings look like a thin line.

Saturn's ring system is very wide. It's spread out over a distance of 175,000 miles (282,000 km). If you traveled that distance from Earth, you would be more than halfway to the moon. Yet the rings are only a few hundred feet thick. That's less than half the length of a football field.

Several of Saturn's moons are labeled in this photograph.

Hyperion

Titan

Rhea

Mimas

Dione

Enceladus

Tethys

CHAPTER 5

Many, Many Moons

Only Jupiter has more moons (63) than Saturn.

Earth has only one moon. But so far, astronomers have found 59 moons orbiting Saturn! And there may be more. With all those moons orbiting the planet, Saturn is a bit like a mini–solar system.

This is a photograph of part of Jupiter with one of its larger moons, Io.

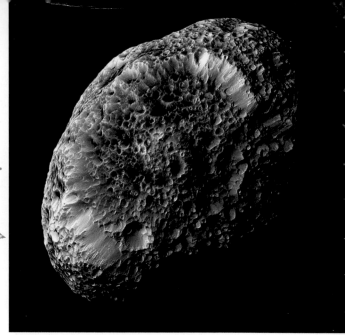

Hyperion looks like a sponge because it has so many craters.

Saturn's moons are made of rock or ice. Many moons have craters, or holes, in their surfaces. These craters were formed when objects such as asteroids crashed into the moons.

Saturn's moons are different from one another. A moon called Enceladus (en-SELL-uh-dis) has volcanoes that spray ice into space. A moon called Hyperion (hy-PEER-ee-un) is known for its strange shape. A moon called Titan (TY-tun) is the second-largest moon in the solar system. There are mountains and sand dunes on its surface.

Meet Four of Saturn's Moons:

Enceladus (en-SELL-uh-dis)
Year discovered: 1789
Size (in diameter):
311 miles (501 km)
Distance from Saturn:
147,500 miles (237,378 km)
Time to orbit Saturn: 33 hours
Interesting fact: Ice sprayed from volcanoes on Enceladus becomes part of Saturn's rings.

Iapetus (eye-AP-eh-tuss)
Year discovered: 1671
Size (in diameter):
892 miles (1,436 km)
Distance from Saturn:
2,212,888 miles (3,561,300 km)
Time to orbit Saturn: 79 days
Interesting fact: Parts of this moon are very bright and parts are very dark.

Mimas (MY-muss)
Year discovered: 1789
Size (in diameter):
242 miles (389 km)
Distance from Saturn:
115,277 miles (185,520 km)
Time to orbit Saturn: 23 hours
Interesting fact: Mimas is one of Saturn's closest moons.

Titan (TY-tun)
Year discovered: 1655
Size (in diameter):
3,200 miles (5,150 km)
Distance from Saturn:
759,220 miles (1,221,846 km)
Time to orbit Saturn: 16 days
Interesting fact: Titan is bigger than the planet Mercury.

On Titan, rain may be made of a liquid similar to gasoline.

This image of Titan was taken from 99,000 miles (159,325 km) away.

Titan is Saturn's largest moon and the second-largest moon in the solar system. It is bigger than Mercury. Titan is like Earth in many ways. Both have mountains, sand dunes, rivers, and lakes. Titan's rivers and lakes aren't filled with water, though. They contain a colorless liquid called methane. Titan may help scientists learn about Earth.

What Titan Can Teach Us

Titan may hold important clues to how life began on Earth. It is one of the few moons in our solar system with an atmosphere. Titan's atmosphere is rich in a gas called nitrogen. Astronomers believe Titan's atmosphere might be similar to what Earth's atmosphere was like billions of years ago.

There are chemicals on Titan that also make it similar to Earth at that time. By studying Titan, astronomers might better understand how Earth changed over the years.

This illustration shows *Voyager 2* orbiting Saturn.

CHAPTER 6

Missions to Saturn

Radio signals from *Cassini* take 1 hour and 20 minutes to reach Earth.

Astronomers have learned a lot about our solar system from space missions. Even far-off Saturn has been looked at up close by four spacecraft. A spacecraft called *Cassini* is still circling the planet!

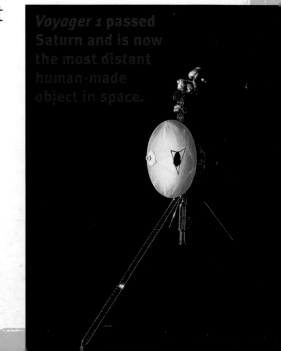

Voyager 1 passed Saturn and is now the most distant human-made object in space.

The first spacecraft to photograph Saturn was *Pioneer 11* in 1979. Before that, astronomers thought Saturn had five rings. *Pioneer*'s close-up pictures revealed a sixth ring.

The next two missions were *Voyager 1*, in 1980, and *Voyager 2*, in 1981. Like *Pioneer 11*, the Voyagers flew past Saturn and went deeper into space. Their photos proved that Saturn had a seventh ring. Astronomers also learned that each "ring" was made up of thousands of smaller rings. They also discovered that Saturn had at least 10 moons.

Cassini-Huygens is about the size of a 30-passenger school bus.

The Cassini Mission

In 1997, Saturn got a spacecraft of its own. The *Cassini-Huygens* (kah-SEE-nee HY-guhnz) craft was sent to explore Saturn and its moons. *Cassini* was the first spacecraft to orbit Saturn, beginning in June 2004. *Huygens* was a small space probe attached to *Cassini*. Its aim was to study the moon Titan.

Cassini and *Huygens* snapped more than 300,000 pictures of Saturn, its rings, and its moons. Using 12 different instruments, *Cassini* conducted 27 scientific investigations. *Cassini* found many more moons orbiting Saturn. The spacecraft will orbit until it runs out of fuel.

An artist drew this picture showing the stages (from left to right) of *Huygens* parachuting toward Titan.

On December 24, 2004, the *Huygens* probe detached from *Cassini*. On January 14, 2005, it released a parachute and drifted down to land on Titan's surface. Instruments on the *Huygens* space probe studied Titan's surface and its thick atmosphere.

Saturn may always be the jewel of our solar system. It is becoming less mysterious, however, as space missions reveal more about the planet and its many rings and moons. ⭐

True Statistics

Classification: Gas giant

Year Galileo first saw the rings through a telescope: 1610

Size: 95 times larger than Earth

Number of moons: 56

Atmosphere: Yes

Atmospheric temperature: −202°F (−130°C)

Distance from the sun: About 886 million mi. (1.4 billion km)

Distance from Earth: About 746 million mi. (1.2 billion km) at its closest point

Distance around planet: About 235,000 mi. (378,000 km)

Did you find the truth?

F Saturn's rings are one solid piece.

T If you tried to stand on Saturn, you would sink into the planet.

Resources

Books

Atkinson, Stuart. *Space Travel*. Austin, TX: Raintree Steck-Vaughn, 2003.

Bailey, Gerry. *Journey into Space*. Minneapolis: Picture Window Books, 2005.

Jackson, Ellen. *The Worlds Around Us: A Space Voyage*. Minneapolis: Millbrook Press, 2006.

Kerrod, Robin. *Asteroids, Comets, and Meteors*. Minneapolis: Lerner Publications, 2000.

Lassieur, Allison. *Astronauts*. Danbury, CT: Children's Press, 2000.

Shearer, Deborah A. *Space Missions*. Mankato, MN: Capstone Books, 2006.

Taylor-Butler, Christine. *Saturn*. Danbury, CT: Children's Press, 2008.

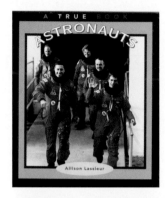

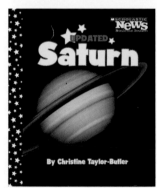

Organizations and Web Sites

NASA Kids' Club

www.nasa.gov/kidsclub
Check out this Web site for fun interactive games.

The Planetary Society

65 North Catalina Avenue
Pasadena, CA 91106-2301
626-793-5100
www.planetary.org
This group is dedicated to exploring the solar system.

Saturn's Ring System

pds-rings.seti.org/saturn
Look here for information on and photos of Saturn's rings.

Places to Visit

Smithsonian National Air and Space Museum

Independence Avenue at 4th Street, SW
Washington, DC 20560
202-633-1000
www.nasm.si.edu
This museum has the world's largest collection of historic spacecraft.

Important Words

asteroids (AS-tuh-roidz) – large pieces of rock that orbit the sun

astronomers (uh-STRAW-nuh-murz) – scientists who study the planets, stars, and space

atmosphere (AT-mu-sfihr) – the blanket of gases that surrounds a planet or moon

axis (AK-siss) – an imaginary line that runs through the center of a planet or other object

chemical (KE-mih-kuhl) – a substance or mixture of substances

comets – large chunks of rock and ice that travel around the sun

equator – an imaginary line around the center of a moon or a planet, halfway between the north and south poles

gravity – a force that pulls two objects together; gravity pulls you down onto Earth

orbit – to travel around an object such as a sun or planet

rotation – the action of spinning on an axis

solar system (SOH-lur SISS-tuhm) – a sun and all the objects that travel around it

Index

About the Author

Award-winning author Elaine Landau has a bachelor's degree from New York University and a master's degree in library and information science from Pratt Institute.

She has written more than 300 non-fiction books for children and young adults. Although Ms. Landau often writes on science topics, she especially likes writing about planets and space.

She lives in Miami, Florida, with her husband and son. The trio can often be spotted at the Miami Museum of Science and Space Transit Planetarium. You can visit Elaine Landau at her Web site: www.elainelandau.com.

PHOTOGRAPHS © 2008: Corbis Images: 16 (Dennis di Cicco), 25 (Warren Faidley), 4 top, 7, 24; Getty Images: cover (Denis Scott), back cover (StockTrek); Masterfile/Chris McElcheran: 23; NASA: 5, 37 (ESA/JPL/University of Arizona), 4 bottom, 41 (JPL), 9, 10, 18, 19, 26, 31, 33, 34, 35 top left, 35 top right, 35 bottom left, 35 bottom right, 42 (JPL/Space Science Institute), 36 (JPL/University of Arizona), 3 (Erich Karkoschka/University of Arizona); Pat Rasch: 14, 15, 17; Photo Researchers, NY: 39 (Atlas Photo Bank), 12 (Julian Baum), 27 center, 32 (John Chumack), 22 (Steve A. Munsinger), 6 (Pekka Parviainen), 27 top (Gianni Tortoli), 28 (Detlev van Ravenswaay); Photri Inc.: 20, 38; Scholastic Library Publishing, Inc.: 44; Smithsonian Institution Libraries: 27 bottom; The Image Works/Mary Evans Picture Library: 11.